IN THE TRACKS OF THE 'ACE'

THE DESTRUCTION OF THE S...
NETWORK WEST OF SALI...

Jeffery Grayer

Noodle Books

© Kevin Robertson (Noodle Books) and Jeffery Grayer 2008

ISBN 978-1-906419-01-1

First published in 2008 by Kevin Robertson under the **NOODLE BOOKS** imprint
PO Box 279
Corhampton
SOUTHAMPTON
SO32 3ZX

www.kevinrobertsonbooks.co.uk

Printed in England by the Alden Press

Front cover: The remoteness of much of the Withered Arm is epitomised in this picture of lonely Camelford station situated up a long hill some 1¼ miles from the small town it served. From here one could catch a connecting Western National bus t Boscastle. The scene is made even more poignant following removal of track and through use of the station building and platform as sack storage by an agricultural merchant. Today the building still stands, though much altered, as the Museum of Historic Cycling.

Preceding page: Waterloo in 1962 sees Merchant Navy Pacific 35018 'British India Line' at the head of the 'ACE' being duly noted in his spotter's notebook by an admiring schoolboy. Today's faceless DMU replacement, which terminates at Exeter, can hardly bear comparison with the former multi-portioned train which provided connections and through coaches to a multitude of destinations in Devon and Cornwall.
                                                                                                                    Les Elsey

Inside rear cover: Steam renaissance! Steam made a triumphant return to the Salisbury - Yeovil route in October 1986 whe 35028 'Clan Line', which is seen here speeding through Sherborne, did the honours with the 'Blackmore Vale Express'. The inauguration of the Yeovil Steam Centre, complete with watering and turning facilities, will doubtless ensure that steam will continue to visit the route well into the future.

Rear cover: Barnstaple Bridge Requiem - this really is the end of the line!

Unless stated otherwise, all photographs are by the Author.

CONTENTS

Seen in 1968, Halwill Junction remains one of several settlements in Britain named after railway facilities even though they have long gone. Due to its transport links, Halwill developed a range of services and could boast at one time a Post Office, Police Station, Bank, Public House, Chapel, small Cottage Hospital, Garage, Cattle Market, an Egg Packing Station and several shops. The station lay derelict for a while but was subsequently demolished and housing built over the site in 1989.

An interesting view of a seldom recorded activity at Lydford Junction taken in early 1969 when chainmen and technical staff were engaged in measuring up and painting identification numbers on pointwork and other useful lengths of track for which BR would be able to find another home elsewhere on the system.   Edward D Hamer

INTRODUCTION

As unmodified Bulleid Pacific 34015 "Exmouth" slowly drew to a stop at Padstow at a little after 5 pm on the afternoon of Saturday 5th September 1964, the end of an era stretching back to 19th July 1926 had come to a close. Earlier in the day 34023 "Blackmore Vale" had left Padstow with the six coaches of the last up ACE, to be joined at Halwill by two coaches from Bude. The withdrawal of the Atlantic Coast Express service was symptomatic of the rapid decline in summer holiday rail travel in the UK experienced in the early 1960s. By its last summer of operation Bude and Torrington sections of this famous multi-portioned express operated only on Saturdays, the Plymouth portion had been withdrawn, leaving just two Monday - Friday destinations of Ilfracombe and Padstow.

My own introduction to the ACE had been 2 years previously at Exeter Central station, where I spent the majority of a family holiday which was ostensibly based at Exmouth. I photographed 35009 "Shaw Savill" taking over one of the up services one August afternoon in 1962.This volume graphically portrays the destruction of the former SR network west of Salisbury following takeover by the WR in 1963. Much has been written about the contribution that this administrative change made to the lines in question but it is probable that had the SR retained control much the same fate would have ultimately befallen this network, given the ethos of the Beeching Report, dependant as it was upon declining summer holiday traffic. By 1963 it was alleged that the SR lines west of Salisbury were failing to cover even their direct costs.

As an example of the parlous state of rural rail finances in the far west, BR estimated the combined income from the Bude and North Cornwall steam operated lines to be just £40,400 in 1963 covering a pathetic 27% of the direct operating costs of £149,445. Passenger surveys were undertaken during three sample weeks (February and July 1963 and March 1964) and the figures provided depressing reading. For example during w/e 16/2/63 a daily average of just 113 passengers joined and 122 alighted from all Monday – Friday trains at all North Cornwall line stations with Bude line trains attracting corresponding daily averages of 300 joining and 267 alighting passengers. Whilst the summer loadings were better, a daily average on one Saturday in July producing figures of 549 joining and 399 alighting (North Cornwall) and 564 joining and 730 alighting (Bude) it must be remembered that the season in North Cornwall is considerably shorter than that enjoyed on the south coast Devon & Cornish Rivieras.

So began a catalogue of rationalisation, withdrawals and closures only partially mitigated in recent years by station re-openings, improvements in motive power and the provision of passing loops to counter the shortsighted singling of double track sections. The images in this book attempt to reflect the changes that have left large areas of the West Country without rail transport and have provided prodigious financial obstacles to any attempts to undo the hasty decisions of previous decades.

Jeffery Grayer. Somerset. February 2008

Following the introduction of Warship Class locomotives to the route by the WR in 1964, they became a common sight at Salisbury working the Waterloo – Exeter semi-fast service. Green liveried D825 "Intrepid" is seen in 1967, when steam infrastructure in the shape of water cranes was still in evidence, on a freight working in the direction of Westbury. D825 lasted in service until August 1972 being scrapped at Swindon in October with the last survivors of the class being withdrawn at the year end. They did not enjoy a good service record on the Exeter route and few passengers were sorry to see them displaced in

1-1-1963	Western Region takeover of ex SR lines west of Wilton.
27-3-1963	Publication of the Beeching Report.
5-9-1964	Last run of the 'ACE'.
7-9-1964	Semi-fast service introduced on Salisbury-Exeter line.
7-3-1966	Closure of intermediate stations on Salisbury-Exeter line. Wilton South, Dinton, Semley, Templecombe, Milborne Port, Chard Junction, Seaton Junction, Broad Clyst, Pinhoe.
4-3-1967	Last run of Brighton – Plymouth through service.

Wilton South was one of nine intermediate stations between Salisbury and Exeter closed from 7th March 1966, closures which were overshadowed by the Somerset & Dorset finale which occurred on the same weekend. The town of Wilton was served by a frequent bus service into the cathedral city and train usage was very low in the final years, a traffic survey of 1963 showing that an average of only 3 passengers travelled daily in an easterly direction into Salisbury, the total of all joining and alighting passengers being just 17. Wilton marked the start of WR territory from 1st January 1963 and, from 2nd April 1967, the beginning of the long single track section to Templecombe. Seen here in 1968 the box was renamed Wilton in October 1973 when it assumed responsibility for the new junction of the ex GWR and SR lines a mile to the east. The box was retained until 29th November 1981 when Salisbury panel took over its functions. However it was dismantled and re-erected on the Mid Hants Railway at Medstead & Four Marks.

April - June 1967	Singling of Wilton – Gillingham, Gillingham – Templecombe, Sherborne - Chard Junction, Chard Junction - Honiton, Honiton - Pinhoe.
10-1967	Sherborne – Yeovil Junction reverted to double line working.
5-1971	Reopening of Sidmouth Junction station as Feniton.
5-1972	Hastings demus introduced on Brighton-Exeter through train.
8-10-1973	Wilton South box took over control of WR line to Westbury.

Dinton also closed in March 1966 but until 1994 the MoD continued to service depots in the area at Chilmark, Baverstock and Dinton by rail, necessitating retention of some two miles of the former up line as a siding to give access to these facilities. The station is seen here in the late 1960s with a few wagons in the yard. In 1948 / 49 over forty time-expired SR locomotives were scrapped by contractors in Baverstock sidings. The wooden construction on the platform is not the signalbox but an old LSWR cabin, the working box being formerly located adjacent to the down line.

1-5-1977	Hastings demus replaced by Class 33s on Brighton – Exeter train.
12-5-1980	Class 50s replace Class 33s on Salisbury –Exeter line with Mk 2 coaching stock.
19-8-1981	Salisbury panel box opened.
1983	Serpell Report published including an option of closing Salisbury – Exeter line.

ollowing singling in April 1967, the platform coping stones at Semley's former down platform were in the process of being moved. The relatively modern replacement signalbox seen on the up platform (just past the end of the canopy) was only ened in January 1961 and along with that at Tisbury had a very short working life, Semley box being taken out of service in ecember 1965 three months before the station itself closed.

6-5-1983	Re-opening of Pinhoe station.
10-1983	Templecombe station re-opened.
4-3-1986	Opening of Tisbury loop at cost of £435k
986	BR restructuring into Network South East (Salisbury – Pinhoe initially then extended to Exeter Central) Inter City, and Regional Railways (Barnstaple and Gunnislake branches).

A down Warship hauled Exeter service rolls into Gillingham up platform which tended to be used for trains in both directions, unless services were required to pass here, as the main station facilities were located on this platform. The recently severed down line can be seen by the bridge in the background, evidence of the short sighted singling of much of the route that took place following the WR takeover. To enable the route to fulfil its potential again in a time of rising passenger numbers it is likely that relaying of the second track will have to be undertaken on much, if not all, of the Salisbury – Exeter line, an exercise likely to run into many hundreds of millions of pounds.

herborne Period Piece - 1960s style. A maroon liveried Warship pulls away with a London service whilst cars and vans of the eriod are held at the crossing gates. A brace of Royal Mail Morris 1000 vans complete the scene. Virtually all has now isappeared, long gone are the Warships; Royal Mail no longer use the trains to handle mailbags and whilst red vans are still ommon the faithful old Morris's have all departed; the crossing gates were replaced by lifting barriers in 1970; and the signalbox as been sold out of BR service.

2-10-1986	Return of steam to Salisbury – Yeovil route with Blackmore Vale Express.
990	Class 47s replaced Class 50s on Salisbury – Exeter line.
2-6-1993	New DMU depot opened at Salisbury, introduction of Class 159 units.

Salisbury to Exeter - SHERBORNE

The driver of Warship D810 "Cockade" leans out of his cab waiting the "right away" from Sherborne with an up train. The typical SR concrete lamp post with hexagonal shade and attendant green totem completes the picture. D810 entered traffic in September 1959 and was withdrawn in November 1971 only to be reinstated three days later. It was one of the last four of the class to remain in service, being finally withdrawn on 3rd December 1972. It almost made it into preservation but D821 "Greyhound", one of the other final quartet, was found to be in better mechanical condition and D810 was duly scrapped at Swindon in September 1973.

Salisbury to Exeter - YEOVIL JUNCTION

During the nine year reign of the Cromptons on the route, an unidentified example gets away from Yeovil Junction station with an up service to Waterloo passing the signalbox, formerly known as "A" box, which still retains its SR green boxplate. This box was in fact briefly closed, following the introduction of singling from Sherborne to Chard Junction on 7th May 1967. However, this was found to be unworkable with lengthy delays to trains resulting, so double track was reinstated between Sherborne and a point just short of Yeovil Junction station on 1st October 1967 and the signalbox was consequently reopened.

ken from the rear carriage of a departing Warship hauled Exeter service in 1968, the severing of the up through road at Yeovil nction is readily apparent. The footbridge still spans all tracks but would subsequently be truncated, in a visually disastrous shion, to serve just the former up platform. There appears to be a number of goods wagons in the up yard. The up branch bay, rmerly used by shuttle trains to Yeovil Town and latterly Pen Mill stations, was not made available to mainline trains until 1975.

995	Seven year Franchise for Salisbury – Exeter route awarded to South West Trains.	
997	Privatisation of British Rail completed.	
003	South West Trains again awarded franchise for Salisbury – Exeter route.	

YEOVIL TOWN & SHED

Although it was the most conveniently sited of all the town's three stations, this did not prevent the closure of Yeovil Town. The station is seen here in 1968 after withdrawal of the Pen Mill – Junction shuttle, which had latterly used the one remaining track through the station, which has already lost its island platform, to gain access to the shed. This track was also used by freight services to Hendford Goods Yard, situated on the former Taunton line but these were withdrawn in May 1968. The track was removed in late 1968 and the site lay derelict until 1971 when it was purchased by Yeovil Borough Council and the remaining buildings demolished in 1973. To the left of the shed stands the small brick built engine cleaner's cabin, and the stone building the left of that did duty as the guard's cabin and housed Mutual Improvement Classes. In earlier years it had also acted as a dormitory for guards working "double home" turns. Passenger services were withdrawn from Yeovil Town in October 1966 and today the area contains a car park and leisure complex.

| 4-9-1965 | Final summer Saturday through train Bude – Paddington via Yeovil Pen Mill |
| 3-10-1966 | Withdrawal of Yeovil Town - Yeovil Junction shuttle service. |

Sunlight slants through the decaying roof of Yeovil Town engine shed (originally coded 72C but latterly 83E). The shed closed to steam in June 1965 but remained open as a signing on point and to house the Yeovil Pen Mill – Yeovil Junction single car DMU shuttle until it was withdrawn from 6th May 1968. Strangely enough even after this date Yeovil continued to supply a crew for the 350 hp diesel shunter which was engaged on track recovery over the former S&D route which at that time had reached as far north as Binegar. The building seen through the left hand arch of the shed was the former enginemen's cabin and shedmaster's office and the footbridge in the distance spans the empty trackbed of the former Taunton line.

Following singling of much of the mainline, Chard Junction became a passing loop with new crossings installed to the north and south of the station. The signalbox seen here resplendent with green signboard in th early 1970s controlled not only this loo but also the level crossing gates adjacent to the station which were replaced with full lifting barriers in January 1968. This old LSWR box was demolished and replaced initially by a temporary box on the opposite side of the line but ultimately by a permanent modern wooden structure on the same site in December 1982.

The former branch platform for the line to Chard Central and Taunton lay behir the up platform and in this view still sported its concrete nameboard. The line to Chard and Taunton closed to passengers in September 1962 and to Chard for freight, latterly tar and molasses, in October 1966 some sever months after closure of the main platforms at Chard Junction. Over the years since there has been pressure to re-open the station but so far to no avai intending rail passengers from Chard and district having to travel to Crewkerr or Axminster. The building just seen in the background is the local hostelry, formerly the Chard Road Hotel and now the Three Counties Inn, which once played host to uninvited guests in the shape of a runaway rake of trucks, the guards van of which ended up in the Lounge Bar !

e scene from the milk sidings at Chard Junction showing the large creamery established in the 1930s by United Dairies. Both
d tankers and rail milk tanks are apparent in this view as is a diesel shunter owned by the dairy and used to shunt wagons
nin its compound. Milk traffic was lost to rail in April 1980 and the up side station buildings seen here were later demolished. It
s hoped to reopen the sidings at the creamery in 1996 but this never materialised.

Salisbury to Exeter - AXMINSTER

From the last carriage of a departing Water[l] service in 1969 it is apparent that Axminste[r] still retains not only its gas lighting but its concrete running in board inviting one to "Change for Lyme Regis Line". Since November 1965 this had no longer been possible with the closure of the branch, intending passengers for the Dorset seasid[e] resort having to take a bus which left from t[he] station forecourt.

Lyme Regis Branch - LYME REGIS

Southern National buses could often be fou[nd] parked up outside the station building at Ly[me] Regis following closure of the line in 1965 a[nd] a couple are seen here. Although not direct[ly] served by the ACE, some of the through coaches from Lyme did become part of the famous train at Salisbury for the onward journey to London. The wooden station building was quietly rotting away in this vie[w] but in 1979 much of it was rescued and re-erected at Alresford on the Watercress Line[to] house a gift and book shop. In the mid 198[0s] much of the site at Lyme was redeveloped [as] a small industrial estate.

3-2-1964	Goods facilities withdrawn fro[m] Lyme Regis
1-3-1965	Single car DMUs introduced.
29-11-1965	Closure of Lyme Regis branc[h]

With the closure of the Seaton branch in March 1966 the raison d'etre of Seaton Junction was gone, there being little in the way f local population to support a train service. The goods yard closed in April 1966 but coal traffic continued until May 1967 with ilk lasting a little longer. The four tracks through the station were reduced to just a single line in June 1967, the former down hrough road being initially retained. In October 1972 the track was slewed to the site of the former up through line.

Salisbury to Exeter - SEATON JUNCTION

From the bucking and swaying last carriage of an Exeter service taken at speed whilst building up momentum for the assault on Honiton Incl ahead, is an easterly view of Seaton Junction showing the former Seaton branch bay on the right.

Seaton Branch - COLYTON

Colyton, one of the two intermediate stations on the Seaton branch, is seen in the period between closure in March 1966 and refurbishment as the northern terminus of the 2'9" gauge Seaton & District Tramway which extended to this point in March 1980.

4-11-1963	DMUs introduced to East Devo branches
7-3-1966	Closure of Seaton branch
28-8-1970	Seaton Tramway opened initial section

the soft evening light even a 3-car DMU, which would ultimately be given the soubriquet "Heritage", manages to provide a
easant image as it climbs Honiton Bank after having just passed through the closed station at Seaton Junction. DMUs were first
roduced to the line by the WR to supplement the initial semi-fast service from Waterloo in 1964, generally following the faster
ins from Salisbury to provide stopping services for the intermediate stations and working through to a variety of destinations
:luding Ilfracombe, Plymouth via Okehampton and Barnstaple Junction. Due to lack of toilet facilities they were not generally
ry popular with longer distance travellers and were withdrawn upon closure of many of the intermediate stations in 1966. In
er years before the introduction of modern Class 159 units, some older Exeter based DMUs saw out their last days on various
:al workings between Salisbury and Exeter.

The old station at Honiton witnesses the departure of an up service in the late 1960s whilst a recently alighted passenger wheeling her bicycle is opting for the easier alternative to the footbridge offered by the boarded crossing seen in the foreground. Gas lighting and green enamel signs complete the period picture. The original station building was unfortunately replaced in the 1990s by a characterless modern structure.

ere were two 5-lever crossing
xes situated between Sidmouth
nction and Ottery St Mary, at
osford Gates and Cadhay Gates.
e remains of the former are seen
the top right view whilst the
ossing gate and red target of the
ter are seen on the lower view.
llowing closure to remaining coal
ffic in May 1967, recovery of track
the branch commenced at
dmouth Junction on 28th May 1968
t was subsequently interrupted by
oding of the River Otter on 10th
y.

The substantial station of Ottery St Mary is seen some three years after closure which took place in March 1967. The crossing gates were operated from a relatively modern platform end signalbox, already demolished, which came into use in November 1955. (Inset - "Tanalised Timber" proclaims the sign on the former goods shed which has been in use as a sawmill since the las goods traffic, coal, was handled.)

vel crossing gates still guard the trackbed in this view of Tipton St John's, junction of the Sidmouth and Exmouth lines. Today e down platform has been demolished as has much of the up platform although the station survives as a dwelling. The gates ve long gone but some gate posts remain in situ.

Sidmouth station is seen prior to the demolition of much of the platform canopy after which most of the site was given over to light industrial use. At 200 feet above sea level and 1 mile from the town centre, this was never a very convenient terminus for the Devon resort and no doubt contributed in later years to the drift of passengers to the much more convenient bus service serving the town centre and sea front.

ewed from Otterton Bridge, yellow gorse frames the attractive station of East Budleigh which served the nearby village of terton and the popular beach at Ladram Bay. The concrete building in the former goods yard served as a store for Silcocks ttle feed. The station building has since been converted into a dwelling and the trackbed made into a lawn.

The march of progress is graphically illustrated in this view of Budleigh Salterton with encroaching development already covering much of the trackbed towards Exmouth. The station building did not survive with housing being built on the site but the goods shed was incorporated into Cash & Carry warehouse.

Although the track has gone, much still remains at Littleham where even a Catch Points board was located by the author in the undergrowth and propped against the level crossing gates to enhance the picture. This board was originally located at the top of the 1 in 50 incline from Exmouth. The entire site was subsequently covered with local authority housing.

e former four platform terminus which also boasted an engine shed is seen in straitened circumstances in the early 1970s as Exeter bound DMU stands at the former No 4 platform which was the only one in use after December 1968. Note the adjacent s station seen on the right housing a couple of Devon General double deckers in the smart livery of the time. In 1975 work mmenced on the construction of a new, much reduced, terminal facility to serve the basic railway, the only one of the LSWR's anch lines to East Devon to survive to the present day. The new building, opened in May 1976, occupies the site of the former tform 2 seen on the right. The remaining parts of the old station were to be swept away in the late 1970s to allow construction a relief road

3-1967	Closure of Sidmouth Jun – Sidmouth / Exmouth branches
69	Exmouth terminus building vacated and let as shops
1976	New station opened at Exmouth

Victorian susceptibilities about allowing the line from Budleigh to be built through Exmouth suburbs necessitated the construction of an expensive viaduct to carry the line to the north of the residential area. Seen in the late 1970s its purpose gone with the closure of the line in March 1967, the structure was subsequently demolished.

The imposing façade of Exmouth terminus is seen in the 1970s prior to construction of a new road on the site 1980. The clock has already gone from the centre of the roof, the building having been vacated by BR in 1969 when conversion to shop units took place. Access to trains was via a passage to the right of the building serving the one remaining platform which housed a ticket kiosk. A fine array of cars and taxis of the period is evident.

aken from a passing train in 1968 Exmouth Junction shed, trackless but still retaining the massive coaling plant and water tank, as formerly coded 72A but latterly 83D under WR control. It closed to steam in June 1965, losing its turntable in 1966, and osing completely in March 1967. It then stood empty until early 1970 when demolition took place, the site lying derelict until 979 when a supermarket was erected. The 85 ft high concrete coaling plant, built in 1927 by the Southern Railway, had to be nocked down piecemeal after an initial attempt by the Royal Marines using explosives in March 1970 failed to dislodge it.

The fearsome 1 in 37 gradient up from St Davids to Central station in Exeter posed few problems for the powerful 2700 hp Class 50 locomotives which were introduced to the Waterloo route in May 1980. No. 50 039 "Implacable", formerly D439, storms up the bank with a London service in 1983, the locomotive lasting in service until 1991.The former Exeter Central "B" signalbox, one of three which served the station area and which closed in February 1970, can be seen on the up platform end. The former up through road, already lifted, was taken out of use in November 1969, with the former down through line following in October 1984.

| 1-3-1965 | Singling of Barnstaple line over bridge near Cowley Bridge Junction on temporary basis following flood damage |
| 15-1-1967 | Permanent singling of Barnstaple line over bridge near Cowley Bridge Junction |

the deep midwinter" a Class 33 stands
the head of an up Waterloo service
mposed of Mk 1 coaching stock in the late
70s at Exeter St Davids. Although more
able than the Warship diesels that they
placed in 1971 they did tend to be
mewhat underpowered for the heavier
ins on the London services and resort to
uble heading was necessary on
casions. The Cromptons lasted until 1980
this route when Class 50s were
roduced along with Mk 2 coaches.

Class 45 hurries a service to Bristol and
e Midlands past Cowley Bridge Junction
nalbox which controlled the divergence of
e ex SR lines to Devon and Cornwall.
llowing floods, the former SR mainline
s effectively singled in November 1965
hough flood relief work was not completed
til 1967. Whilst the ex GWR line was
nited to 90 mph the ex SR line had a
vere 25 mph speed restriction imposed.
owley Bridge box lasted until the
roduction of the Exeter MAS scheme
nich began with the Cowley Bridge –
rediton section on 16 December 1984 and
as completed on 5th May 1985.

A Barnstaple bound DMU on the former double track section from north of Cowley Bridge to Copplestone rattles through the request stop of Newton St Cyres without pausing. The line to Crediton was singled in December 1984 and the wooden station building seen on the up platform, the only one remaining in use today, has of course been replaced by the inevitable "bus shelter".

rediton signalbox looks particularly smart in this 1969 view with its new coat of brown and cream paint although the angle of the imney might give some cause for concern! The level crossing gates were not replaced with lifting barriers until 1974. Crediton pplanted Coleford Junction as the junction for the Okehampton and Barnstaple lines in October 1971 when the former down e became a single line to Meldon Quarry with the up line becoming a single line for the North Devon route. Although today its maphore signals have gone Crediton survives as a fringe box to Exeter panel.

Although trains still call at Yeoford, this is only on request and is a far cry from its former interchange role in the days of steam when some expresses from London were divided here for North Devon and for Plymouth and North Cornwall. All buildings seen in this late 1960s view have been demolished except for a small wooden structure on the former up platform. Remains of the once extensive yards, which handled much traffic in cattle, agricultural produce and equipment and which closed in 1964, can be seen on the right.

s an epitaph for the declining fortunes of the line, the setting sun at Yeoford illuminates the tracks. Almost incredibly the building the left housed a Refreshment Room until 1950 to cater for the needs of interchange passengers.

Conversation piece at Copplestone. The half dozen or staff outside the signalbox are probably there in connection with the recently severed former up line which was taken out of use as part of the singling of the route undertaken in October 1971 at which time the 10 lever box was closed. Doubling of the Barnstaple route, completed in 1883 from Coleford Junction, reached as far north as Copplestone whence it remained single as far as Umberleigh once the GWR and LSWR had agreed not to develop their respective routes to Barnstaple. However, the necessary engineering works were completed for double track. The main station building has since been fenced off from the platform being privately owned.

father's Morris Oxford saloon, 68 FPX, which I had borrowed to undertake a tour of lines in North Devon, stands in the yard
Lapford in 1968. A couple of milk tank wagons can be seen in the sidings of the Ambrosia milk product facility located here
m 1928 until 1970. Following closure the building was split into a number of small units, the major one of which housed
ricultural fertiliser which continued to receive deliveries by rail until 1993. The station building was subsequently sold.

3-4-1966	Portsmouth Arms signal box taken out of use.
28-8-1969	Replacement signal box into use at Eggesford following flood damage to original.
30-11-1969	Lifting barriers into use at Eggesford.
3-5-1971	Barnstaple line south of Copplestone singled.
21-5-1971	Barnstaple 'B' box closed.
21-5-1971	Umberleigh signal box closed. Line north of this point singled.
27-1-1974	Lifting barriers replace gates at Crediton.

ft - Taken from the former down platform at Lapford, the ain station building, now sporting the ubiquitous bus shelter, seen through the arches of the A377 bridge. The far right ch which was infilled, together with an adjacent wooden lding, once served in the capacity of a slaughterhouse. This s now been demolished and the arch re-opened.

ght - An unusual feature of Lapford was the staggering of the and down platforms separated as they were by the A377 d bridge. This view from the top of the platform steps shows t the rusting track alongside the island platform, which viously served only down trains, has already been taken out use. The use of two platforms ended in about 1970 when the p was converted into a siding, the platform being molished and the running line slewed to give a straight run tween the bridge seen in the distance and the A377 bridge.

Left - Framed by the guard of a loco hauled Exeter train, a scene which has now vanished from the railways is acted out. On the platform is a barrow piled high with mailbags whilst at the side of the station is the traditional red Royal Mail van which has just delivered its load.

9-1981	Barnstaple - Paddington through summer Saturday service ceased.
Summer 1982	Last through workings Barnstaple - Waterloo (SO).
Summer 1982	Alternate Barnstaple trains DMU / Class 31 haulage. Saturdays only.
30-3-1985	Cowley Bridge signal box closed. (Exeter MAS scheme.)
3-86 to 10-87	'Skipper' and 'Pacer' units used but rigid wheelbase found to be unsatisfactory. Replaced by single car '153' units.
1-11-1987	Barnstaple 'A' box closed.
1-12-1987	Eggesford signal box closed. Token cupboards into use.

ft - King's Nympton station seen in the soft evening light with gas lamps, signalbox, semaphores and passing loop to enhance e bucolic scene. In common with many of the wayside stations on this line the village of the same name was some miles away hough it had originally been named South Molton Road which was even further away at some nine miles distance. The nalbox closed in 1970 when the line was singled and the down platform taken out of use.

ove - A timeless scene that was once common at rural stations up and down the country. The half open Booking Office door, e SR green sign, timetable board and letter box are all part of the pleasant wayside halt of Portsmouth Arms named after the rl of Portsmouth who lived at nearby Eggesford House. There is no village to provide traffic situated as it is in the depths of al Devon. Unfortunately the station building is no more having been replaced by a faceless "bus shelter".

Exeter to Barnstaple - PORTSMOUTH ARMS

A Barnstaple bound 3 car DMU slows fo the Portsmouth Arms stop but the platfo appears devoid of custom. Although the passing loop together with the signalbox was taken out of use in April 1966 the typical SR concrete running in boards remained at the time of this picture but rendered in stark white and black rather than the traditional SR colours.

Exeter to Barnstaple - UMBERLEIGH

Umberleigh station complete with Southern green enamel sign, rhododendron bushes and characteristic LSWR signal box basks in the lengtheni shadows of a late summer evening. This shot was taken shortly before the signal box closed and the passing loop remove as part of signalling and track rationalisation undertaken in 1971 in an attempt to improve the economies of the line. Fortunately the Exeter – Barnstaple route is still with us marketed under the "Tarka Line" banner.

e passing loop at Umberleigh has
cently been removed in this view
though the signalbox was still standing
ly to be subsequently demolished.
mberleigh opened in 1854 and formed
rt of the broad gauge Taw Valley
tension to Barnstaple. The pleasant
untryside around this station remains
changed and was no doubt a
ntributory factor in deciding to base a
liday Camping Coach here for many
ars.

apelton, last stop before Barnstaple,
ways had a rather sparse service and is
en here in 1971. The double track section
no longer in use although the track has
t yet been lifted. The station still sports
green signboard albeit not on the
erational platform.

The junction trackwork of the diverging Torrington and Ilfracombe lines is graphically portrayed in these views of Barnstaple Junction, the latter being taken from the Sticklepath Road bridge. Judging by the smoke issuing from the chimney the signalman of "B" box, previously known as West Box until 1949, has a good fire going to ward off the winter chill. At this date, 1970, most of the infrastructure at the junction is still complete including the footbridge and much of the signalling. B box was taken out of use in May 1971.

much reduced facility at Barnstaple Junction is seen in this 1982 view. Stopblocks have truncated the former middle road and a all bulldozer has been busy clearing the remains of the Ilfracombe branch junction. A Class 31 locomotive runs round its four 1 coaches prior to return to Exeter for, during this summer, the Saturday train service was provided by a mixture of loco- uled stock and DMU's. The bulk of the remaining track was lifted and today just a single line serves the one remaining platform plain Barnstaple, the station having lost its Junction suffix in 1971. Note the Western National bus, providing a connection to nton, waiting in the yard.

1964	Introduction of full DMU service on Ilfracombe line
-12-1967	Singling of Barnstaple - Ilfracombe line.

ft - Barnstaple Bridge, the major engineering work on the Ilfracombe line, carried the railway over the River Taw on 17 pairs of ought iron girders on a 7½ chain radius curve requiring the provision of the continuous check rail seen here. Opened to traffic 1874 it became an eyesore after closure but was not demolished until the summer of 1977, much to the chagrin of local hermen for whom it was a most convenient perch, leaving just a few fragments of the piers visible at low tide.

ove - An Ilfracombe DMU disturbs the local seagull population as it crosses the Taw Bridge during 1970, the final year of eration. Note the white insulators carrying the telegraph wires fitted to the side of the bridge. Originally it had been planned to ntinue to serve the north bank of the Taw with a platform built at The Strand, much more conveniently situated for the town ntre than Barnstaple Junction, after the rest of the Ilfracombe line had closed. Building a new platform rather than continuing to e Barnstaple Town station would have removed the need for two manned level crossings. The Strand also had the benefit of eing adjacent to the town's bus station. In the event presumably the state of the viaduct precluded this plan and the remaining xeter service was cut back to the Junction necessitating a considerable walk to the town for rail passengers ever since.

6-9-1970	Last through Ilfracombe - Paddington train.
-10-1970	Closure of Barnstaple - Ilfracombe line.
975	Barnstaple - Ilfracombe track lifted following abortive preservation scheme.

Barnstaple Town station with its unusual overlapping crossing gates, caused by the fact that the width of the road was greater than the width of the railway track, was closed in 1970 along with the line to Ilfracombe. The signalbox, which was the only block post to remain in operation until closure, subsequently acted as a museum for a while for the Lynton & Barnstaple Railway Preservation Society echoing the station's association with the narrow gauge line which ran from the bay platform here until closure in 1935. The station building did duty as an Indian restaurant after closure until 1994.

e weeds are growing apace along the
ck at Barnstaple Town during that five
ar period, 1970 – 1975, when it was
ed that a preservation attempt might be
ccessful. In the event it was not and,
owing the passage of an inspection train
26th February 1975 hauled by a Class
diesel locomotive, scrap contractors
ved onto the line in October 1975.

e one operational platform at Wrafton is
en during the last year of the line's life,
box having been reduced to level
ssing ground frame status following
gling of the line in 1967.

Tony Woodforth collection

Barnstaple to Ilfracombe - **VELLATOR CROSSING**

Above left - Seen from the window of a departing Ilfracombe DMU in 1970, the last year of operation, proximity of Wrafton station, box and crossing to RA Chivenor seen in the background can be readily appreciated. The RAF took over here in 1939 from th North Devon Airport, which had opened in 1934 flyin to Lundy, the Channel Islands and Cardiff. So whilst not in the same league as Gatwick or Southampton Airport Parkway for example, Wrafton could claim to be one of the first of the SR's rail/air interchange stations !

Above right - Wrafton Signalbox is seen in a parlous state after a fire had consumed much of the wooden structure. The crossing gates can be glimpsed throug the glassless windows lying abandoned at the side o the former trackbed which still retains its ballast. Apa from blistered paint the 17 lever frame seems to hav survived unscathed. The signal box had been reduce to ground frame status in December 1967 following singling of the line.

above - An unidentified Warship locomotive has charge of a 3 coach Ilfracombe train which is seen signalled away at Braunton. After dieselisation a Summer Saturday through train, 1V87, was provided in 1965 from Paddington to Falmouth leaving at 1130 with a portion for Ilfracombe arriving at 1600, the fastest ever London direct service to the North Devon resort, even beating the former Pullman "Devon Belle" service by 60 minutes.

lower left - Vellator Crossing, seen after singling of the line, spanned the minor road from the main A361 to the wetlands of Braunton Marsh. Both signal posts were positioned on the down side, for ease of sighting, the down signal carrying the Vellator home and Braunton distant whilst the up signal comprised the Vellator home and Braunton distant.

Both Tony Woodforth collection

Above - Shot from an Ilfracombe service departing Braunton from the former up line, which was used by all trains after singling in 1967, the station is still substantially intact and even retains a platform barrow to cater for any traffic offering. But the good times of peak holiday traffic, Braunton being billed as the station " For Saunton Sands and Croyde Bay", would never come again. After singling, the signalbox retained only basic equipment to protect the level crossing, all block instruments being removed and all point levers being rendered spare.

Right - A distant signal keeps its lonely vigil beside the deserted trackbed of the Barnstaple - Ilfracombe line near Braunton. Perhaps the absence of a signal ladder has deterred would-be souvenir hunters for the signal still retains its finial and signal arm.

e riot of colour covering the trackbed at Braunton almost masks the set of rusty tracks remaining on the former up side. The e was left in situ until 1975 to allow the North Devon Railway Co., who had an office in Barnstaple, time to raise funds for its rchase, BR having quoted a price of £410,000. Sadly only £20,000 was raised by a share issue and the company went into uidation, the money raised being used to pay legal expenses.

Right - The remains of Stoney Bridge crossing which still sports an LSWR lattice signal post. There were a number of such manned crossings in the short stretch between Braunton and Mortehoe stations and no less than eleven on the whole 15 mile branch which of course did little for the economics of the line's operation. The box contained a six lever frame although the gates remained hand operated until the end

Lower - The signal arms and crossing gates at Heddon Mill Crossing, between Braunton and Mortehoe, still protect the minor road running from the A361 towards Georgeham. The crossing keeper's house remains but the box in which there was an 8 lever frame has been demolished. Six of the levers were for signals, subsequently reduced to four – two home and two distant in each direction, one for a crossover taken out in 1922 and one for the gate lock, the gates being worked by hand until closure.

The Ilfracombe line was singled in December 1967 as part of a rationalisation designed to cut costs, conductor-guards being introduced in September the following year. Unfortunately this only delayed the inevitable with closure coming in October 1970. In the last year of the line's life a 3-car DMU climbs the 1 in 40 gradient of Mortehoe bank with an Ilfracombe train against a background of gathered-in corn in the fields. There were just five services/day each way Mondays-Fridays and seven on summer Saturdays by the end. No trains left the terminus between 1050 and 1528 on Mondays-Fridays, hardly a level of service to encourage the travelling public. The year before closure BR claimed that revenue covered just 14% of total expenses allocated to the line, although income was just sufficient to cover movement costs.

Tony Woodforth collection

Taken shortly after closure the grass grown track and dilapidated building of Mortehoe & Woolacombe station graphically portra
the story of the decline of the SR West Country lines. Track was finally removed in 1975 and the station subsequently became a
childrens' themepark which included four old Mk 1 coaches parked between the former platforms.

Exeter bound DMU tops the bank out
Ilfracombe and passes beneath the
231 overbridge to the north of
ortehoe station. Apart from the
ddington train, all local services by the
t year, 1970, were through trains to
eter St Davids only, just one train
ing on up the incline to the former SR
tion at Exeter Central on summer
turdays. The bridge was subsequently
noved as part of a road junction
alignment.

is panoramic view descending the 1 in
incline into Ilfracombe was taken from
e of the five daily DMU services which
mprised the final timetable. The
posed site of the terminus high above
e town is readily apparent, no doubt
e of the reasons for its declining
pularity with holidaymakers during the
al years of the line. Full DMU working
as introduced in September 1964 but
either this nor track rationalisation and
affing reductions were ultimately able to
ve the line.

Reduced to its final "basic railway" form, Ilfracombe plays host to an Exeter bound DMU service during its final year. Ground frames were installed at each end of the run round loop, thus permitting the continued operation of locomotive hauled trains, but most of the extensive carriage sidings formerly on the left were taken out of use upon closure of the signalbox in December 1967. The final Summer Saturday through train to London, Paddington not Waterloo of course by this time, ran on 26th September 1970 departing Ilfracombe at 1355 hauled by Warship Class D810 "Cockade"

is buffer stop view taken
er closure shows the
oden screen on the right
ich was installed in about
92 to afford some protection
m the westerly gales which
icted this exposed site. A
ffic survey of May 1963
ealed that the Exeter –
acombe passenger service
nerated only £150k in
nual revenue but cost £485k
operate.

e Ilfracombe site seen after
ck removal. The BR Board
tially applied to Ilfracombe
uncil for planning
rmission to erect a holiday
alet centre on the site but
e application was deferred
nding negotiations to reopen
e line by the local
eservation society. In the
ent this came to nought, as
d BR's plans, and the site
as sold to Pall Europe who
bsequently erected a factory
r the production of high
ade medical filters.

Crediton to Okehampton - BOW

With its village over one mile away to the no along a minor road, Bow never attracted gre passenger custom and after 1964 became a unstaffed halt but continued to be served by the Okehampton shuttle until the end of the service in 1972. It is seen here, prior to singling of the route in October 1971, playing host to a single car DMU departing for Okehampton.

Crediton to Okehampton - NORTH TAWTON

North Tawton's grandiose station was seemingly out of all proportion to the meagre passenger traffic offering being similarly disadvantaged in its positioning some 1¼ miles from its village. Following the introduction of conductor-guards to the route in September 1968 the station lost its remaining staff. The footbridge and down sid waiting shelter seen here were dismantled fo subsequent re-erection at Ropley on the Mid Hants Railway.

ampford Courtenay is seen in 1969. This was the third name bestowed on this seemingly insignificant stop on the SR's ainline to Plymouth. As it had been the terminus of the line for nearly five years it initially qualified for the title "Okehampton ad"(1867-1871). Upon extension to Okehampton it became "Belstone Corner" (1871-1872), adopting its final name in 1872. e few houses clustering around the red telephone box seen in the background constituted the only habitation in the mediate proximity, the village again being some distance away.

6-1972	Closure of Yeoford - Okehampton line to passengers.
997	Okehampton – Exeter reopened for special trains. Services also operate from Okehampton – Meldon Viaduct (Dartmoor Railway)

Crediton to Okehampton - SAMPFORD COURTENAY

A single line traversed by a few stone trains was all that was left at Sampford Courtenay fo many years. After withdrawal of passenger services in 1972, the building seen here was eventually demolished but in May 2004 the Dartmoor Railway re-opened the station and i the summer of 2007 one could alight here fro one of the five trains that ran each way betwe Exeter and Okehampton on Sundays.

Crediton to Okehampton - OKEHAMPTON

Mailbags outnumber passengers in this view an Exeter bound service at Okehampton in th winter of 1971. The single car units which operated the Okehampton service latterly had suffered a spate of failures the previous winte with Hymeks and Warships stepping into the breach hauling either the failed units or with a solitary BSK in tow.

Exeter service waits at Okehampton in the rain in 1971, the year before withdrawal, comprising a single car DMU the ...instay of the branch in latter years. Mailbags are being loaded from the platform barrow and the connecting coach to Bude ...its in the yard outside. The suffix "Alight here for Shebbear College" mentioned on the running in board used to adorn the ...tion at Dunsland Cross on the Bude line, closed in October 1966, which at 5 miles distance was much nearer to the school ...n Okehampton some 15 miles away. The Bude rail replacement coach operated by Jennings of Bude consisted initially of six ...urn journeys daily, seven in summer, from the railhead at Okehampton, a subsidy being paid for the first two years until the ...te became self supporting. Following closure of Okehampton station the coach from Bude ran through to Exeter St Davids ...d Exeter Bus Station. In 1999 a new "Atlantic Coast Express" (bus service) was launched by the First Western National group, ...X9 starting from Bude and serving Bridgerule, Holsworthy and Halwill Junction and the X10 starting from Boscastle serving ...melford and Launceston before combining at Okehampton and onwards to Exeter.

In 1966 one could still change at Okehampton for Bude and the North Cornwall line, a single car Bude train is seen waiting in the bay platform which in previous years would have played host to perhaps a T9, Maunsell mogul or Standard tank. Today Okehampton station has been restored to its former glory and the Dartmoor Railway operate services to Meldon Quarry and southwards to Sampford Courtenay with occasional workings to Exeter on summer weekends. There is a plan to open a Park and Ride facility at Okehampton and reintroduce a commuter rail service, to relieve the traffic choked A30 into Exeter.

Mike Radfo

book on the SR lines in the West Country
uld be complete without a view of their major
gineering feature – Meldon Viaduct. Seen here
1968 from an unusual viewpoint the seemingly
ndly nature of the structure is apparent.
lowing concern about the condition of the
duct, working was confined to one track from
ril 1966 until closure of the Okehampton –
re Alston route in May 1968 after which time it
s used as a quarry headshunt until the late
30s. At one point steel decking and a roadway
re laid to allow lorries to cross during
nstruction of Meldon Reservoir which was
mpleted in 1972. All remaining track was
lly lifted in 1990. After expenditure of
50,000 the viaduct was refurbished in 1996
d, at the grand old age of 133 years, carries
lkers and cyclists as part of the Dartmoor Way
tpath and Devon Coast to Coast Cycle path.

ck recovery between Bere Alston and Meldon
gan in September 1969, D838 "Rapid" being
ed on a demolition train on October 30. The
rk was completed by the following summer and
ging by the lack of vegetation on the ballast at
destowe the gangs have only recently passed
ugh. Today the space between the platforms
s been infilled to make a lawn for an extended
tion house.

Sheltering in a hollow from the worst of the Dartmoor weather lies the attractive station of Brentor. In the lower picture sleeper indentations in the former up trackbed can still be seen in this view of Brentor taken in 1970 from the overbridge just two years after the last passenger trains ran. The trackbed of the ex GWR line to Launceston, which was closed to passengers during that infamous snowstorm at the end of December 1962 can be seen on the far right. Snow intervened again in the story of railways in this area in February 1969 when some 9 months after closure to passengers, the former SR line at Brentor again echoed to the sound of at least four different trains when owing to a breach in the sea wall near Starcross and snow blocking the WR mainline between Plymouth and Totnes, Warship Class D865 "Zealous" with snow ploughs attached was sent out to clear the former up road of the closed line between Bere Alston and Meldon. The following day the operation was repeated and D827 "Kelly" followed on hauling a freight train as far as Brentor where it expired and had to be rescued by Western Class D1018 "Western Buccaneer". Perversely the LSWR and GWR chose to serve two different settlements on their parallel lines between Lydford and Tavistock, Brentor and Marytavy & Blackdown a mile or so to the south. The overbridges over both routes at Brentor were demolished in 1989 and the road widened but fortunately the station house was converted into a most attractive dwelling retaining many features from its former life and offering bed and breakfast accommodation.

folly of closing the Okehampton – Bere Alston section of the former SR mainline in 1968 was later compounded by allowing velopment on the trackbed at Tavistock North seen here a year or so after closure. The erection of houses and Council offices mean that any projected re-opening of the line from Tavistock to Bere Alston will necessarily be restricted to a station on the skirts of the town. Fortunately the elegant footbridge was rescued by the Plym Valley Railway with the up side station canopy ding a home at the Launceston Steam Railway.

4-1966	Tracks over Meldon Viaduct singled
-1964	St Budeaux – Devonport closed completely
-1968	Closure of Okehampton – Bere Alston line
-1970	St Budeaux – Bere Alston singled

This could easily have been the view from a service arriving from Okehamp[ton] prior to May 1968 but is in fact that tak[en] from a service from Gunnislake in earl[y] 1970 when trains from Gunnislake ran behind the signalbox situated on the u[p] platform to gain the former down main and then reversed into the station for their onward journey to Plymouth. This line was singled as far as St Budeaux [in] September 1970 and the signalbox closed although the green running in board still proclaims this as the junctio[n] for the Callington Branch.

The final layout at Bere Alston with jus[t] single line at the former down platform[.] The remains of the footbridge stairs ar[e] still apparent on the former up platform[.] which also houses the closed signalbo[x.] The area to the right contained three sidings which remained in situ until the end of 1968 although freight traffic had finished in February 1966.

The 12 arch Calstock Viaduct spans the Devon/Cornwall border, represented by the River Tamar flowing below, carrying the erstwhile line to Callington which was shortened to terminate at Gunnislake in November 1966. The one ton concrete blocks which make up the viaduct were cast on site. A steam operated wagon hoist which replaced a 1 in 6 incline up from the quay, was itself dismantled in 1934, but was situated next to the second arch from the left in this view.

When you realise that the engineer in charge of upgrading the former East Cornwall Mineral Railway in 1907/8 was the redoubtable Colonel Stephens, the somewhat unusual corrugated iron construction of the station building at Calstock, which would not be out of place on the Kent & East Sussex Railway, becomes readily explicable. The remaining buildings on the platform comprise a Gents, Lamp Room and Coalshed. The two goods loops formerly to the left of the station were removed in August 1966 but a solitary isolated van remains in this view. A passing loop was situated here until taken out of use in May 1968.

11-1966   Closure of Callington – Gunnislake section

A train from Plymouth rolls into Gunnislake in the late 1960s, the green and cream station building being similar to the basic design of that provided at Calstock. After closure of the Callington extension arrivals and departures used different platforms here until May 1968, but by the time of this view just one platform was in use.

The mists have rolled down from the moors to enhance this atmospheric view of the buffer stops at Gunnislake. A DMU awaiting return to Bere Alston and Plymouth can be glimpsed through the murk at a platform now devoid of its former buildings and provided with only the standard "bus shelter". In 1994 the station was resited on the east side of an adjacent roadbridge to enable a restriction on HGVs to be lifted.

Callington Branch - CALLINGTON

Even by the date of my visit in 1968 there was precious little left at Callington, beyond a collection of moribund sheds and a length of platform with concrete fencing and a signboard, to show that there was ever a railway presence here. The site was subsequently cleared and now forms the – yes you've guessed it - Beeching Way Industrial Park !

Okehampton to Plymouth - PLYMOUTH FRIARY

Closure of Plymouth Friary to passengers came as far back as September 1958 when it assumed the role of the city's main goods station. Demolition of the buildings came in 1976 and after lying derelict the site was cleared in the early 1990s for housing development. This unusual 1968 view shows a train of Army vehicles waiting on the middle road at the former terminus.

addaford Moor Halt for Thorndon Cross" proclaims the SR concrete signboard at this lonely outpost on the fringe of Dartmoor.
ened in 1926 to serve a proposed health resort at Thorndon Cross which failed to materialise it managed to cling to life until
e closure of the line in October 1966. In this view, taken in 1968, the coping stones, always a valuable commodity, have
eady been removed to reveal the typical "harp" platform construction produced by the Exmouth Junction Concrete Works.

Halwill Junction is a forlorn sight with the track removed in this 1968 view. The level crossing gates lasted a little longer as did the buildings in the former yard but all were ultimately swept away for a housing development appropriately called "Stationfields".

emnants of the once busy summer crowds wait patiently on the up platform at Halwill Junction in 1966 for an Okehampton train oviding onward connections for Exeter and the east. Following withdrawal of the ACE in 1964, an attempt to cater for the indling summer holiday traffic, a through train from Paddington – Bude had been provided in 1965 but did not feature in the netable for the following year, long distance passengers having to make do with a through service to and from Exeter Central nning fast to Okehampton and omitting a couple of stops between Okehampton and Bude. Diesel multiple units took over rvices in this area from 4th January 1965, the single car on the opposite platform forming a Bude working with a train from adebridge seen arriving into the bay platform.

Mike Radford

Plenty of staff but few passengers wishing to travel on one of the North Cornwall line trains seen in the bay platform at Halwill Junction during 1966. By this time just 3 services daily comprised the "Emergency Service" to Wadebridge, with a short working to Launceston on Saturdays, and one even had to change at Wadebridge, onto a service from Bodmin Road, in order to reach the end of the line at Padstow.

Mike Radfor

en from a departing Bude service, a Wadebridge train lurches off to the left at Halwill Junction taking the North Cornwall route. ese trains were scheduled to depart within 1 minute of each other and could often be photographed together. Note the newly d concrete sleepers at the junction, a sure sign, cynics would say, along with repainting of station buildings, of impending sure!

Mike Radford

Above - The waterlogged trackbed of the former Bude branch seen at Whitstone & Bridgerule in 1968 has subsequently been infilled to make a garden for the station building which has been converted into a house.

Opposite – From the state of the weed strewn track one could be forgiven for thinking that the branch to Bude had already clos were it not for the fact that a single car DMU is lurking disconsolately under the canopy of this North Cornwall terminus. The picture graphically illustrates the parlous state into which this former branch had fallen by 1966, the last year of operation. Of course there was no longer any need to run round with DMUs operating and in the absence of freight traffic, which had always been light and was withdrawn from 7 September 1964, it is not surprising that rusty track was well in evidence, but the general of neglect of a dying railway is all pervading. One can only surmise what regenerative effect the "surfing boom" of later years would have had upon the fortunes of this line which always enjoyed better passenger usage than the Wadebridge route from Okehampton and even in the "Emergency Service" warranted 8 return services daily. Mike Radford

The impressive exterior of Bude station, finished in red brick and Portland stone, is seen after closure. It once boasted a refreshment room for the hordes of summer visitors. The building was later demolished and the inevitable housing estate built on the site, one of the roads being named Bulleid Way which I suppose makes a change from Beeching Close !

Much of the steam infrastructure is still visible in this view of Bude taken in the summer of 1966. Working on the assumption that services to Bude and Wadebridge would be withdrawn in March 1966, the WR Timetable for 1966/67 contained no information for these lines and many intending passengers no doubt assumed that they had already closed. In the event closure was deferred until October 3 1966 and an "Emergency Service" timetable had to be instituted.   Mike Radford

...ole for Black Torrington. Hard to believe but on occasions when snow blocked the mainline near Okehampton, the ACE was ...verted via Bideford and the branch to Halwill Junction and could be seen passing through Hole. A fine sight it must have been ...r a station which normally only saw two one-coach passenger trains per day in each direction.

3-1965	Closure of Torrington – Halwill line	
10-1965	Closure of Torrington – Barnstaple line	
1966	Track lifted Halwill - Meeth	

Platform end water cranes, which were the only ones on the route from Torrington, and point levers survive in this picture of Hatherleigh station which although inconveniently sited a mile from the town centre was still the main station on the line warranting a stationmaster for much of its life.

Meeth Halt retains its green signboard in this 1969 view looking up the 1 in 50 grade towards the site of the ungated level crossing over which there was a 5 mph restriction. Following closure of the line in March 1965 track between Halwill Junction and Meeth ball clay works had been removed by March 1966, clay continuing to be taken out northwards from Meeth works until August 1982 and from nearby Marland Works until mid September.

number of halts were provided on the grandly named North Devon & Cornwall Junction Light Railway from Torrington to Halwill nction, some more conveniently sited than others. This is Yarde Halt where the track appears to be well used by clay trains m the nearby workings at Meeth and Marland.

-10-1978	Milk traffic from Torrington ceased
-8-1982	Clay traffic from Torrington branch ceased
84	Tracklifting on Torrington branch

Torrington station photographed in 1968 presents a neat appearance with milk traffic evident on the track leading through the goods shed in the right foreground. Rail borne milk traffic had for long been part of the railway scene until being finally abandoned by BR, a large proportion of this traffic beginning its journey to creameries and to the metropolis on country branch lines such as this, making connection at junction stations with main line express freights. At this time clay and other goods traffic were also handled at Torrington. However, milk was finally lost in 1978 although clay traffic continued until September 1982. Although the passenger service from Torrington to Barnstaple had been withdrawn in October 1965, the section to Bideford was briefly re-opened in January 1968 following the collapse of a section of the road bridge spanning the River Torridge in Bideford. The only practicable route by public transport from the east bank to the west bank of the town was by train to Torrington thence bus back to Bideford. A DMU driving trailer and a newspaper van hauled by D6336, the only suitable stock available at Barnstaple Junction, the Exeter route having been cut by flooding, was provided initially until the Exeter line re-opened on 13th January after which a single railcar was used. The service was free of charge and 10 journeys per day each way were operated for the period of the emergency. A final public passenger train, topped and tailed with Class 31 locomotives, ran from Bristol to Torrington on 6th November 1982 with the last recorded passengers, local officials on a fact finding tour, being carried by a single railcar on 27th January 1983.

A trio of period cars, an 1100 saloon and estate plus a Mk 3 Cortina, are delayed by the passage of a train at Instow gates in the early 1970s hauled by a Class 25 with clay hood wagons in tow. The signalman can just be discerned exchanging the tablet with the driver. This scene has been partially recreated with the restoration of Instow box, dating from 1872 and the first such structure to be afforded Listed Building (Grade II) status, and by the provision of replica gates together with a short length of track on what is now a cycle trail. Due to the prohibitive cost of upgraded trackwork, necessary to handle modern clay vehicles which were urgently needed to replace the old clay hood wagons, clay traffic finished in 1982 and now goes by road.

Instow station is still substantially complete even down to the trio of fire buckets in this 1969 view albeit the passing loop, which was taken out of use in November 1968, has been removed. The building survives today minus canopy and up platform as a local yacht club headquarters. The down platform is still in situ with seats and recreated station signs.

Above - Although partial demolition has been undertaken at Fremington, the unusually tall signalbox remains. The box continue in use until 3rd November 1968 when the loop was taken out of use and two ground frames installed. Only concrete sleepers an chairs constitute the former down line through the station which continued to handle rail borne freight, particularly clay, for the nearby Fremington Quay until the end of 1969, over 14,000 tons of clay having been despatched by sea during that year.

Right - Following "In the tracks of the ACE" which had passed this way just two years before - the last remnant of a once prou railway service in the shape of a solitary single car DMU presents a rather pathetic sight as it makes its lonely way southwards from Halwill Junction. In three months time even this would be history. At this time crossing loops still existed at Launceston, Egloskerry and Camelford on the North Cornwall line but only Halwill had any booked crossings.

Mike Radford

The valley of the River Carey no longer resounds to the bark of a T9, Bulleid Pacific or even the brash horn of a DMU. Ashwater 214 miles from Waterloo, once enjoyed the luxury of the ACE which in 1963/4 called at 10:12 up, with arrival at Waterloo at 15:? and 15:44 down arriving at Padstow at 17:21. Although empty in this view the station is now a private residence.

orth Cornwall Line - EGLOSKERRY

green Morris Minor is parked on the
mer up platform at Egloskerry which
ains its concrete running in board which
still there today although the inter-
tform space has now been infilled.
dly the crossing gates, incidentally the
y pair on the North Cornwall route
tween Halwill and Wadebridge, are
eady gone together with the signalbox.
1964, the ACE no longer called here,
ng non stop between Launceston and
erham.

orth Cornwall Line - TRESMEER

hough situated in the attractively named
mlet of Splatt, the LSWR wisely decided
call this station after a village one mile
ay – Tresmeer. The vegetation growing
the trackbed is its own testament to the
e of the line. The down ACE only called
re on Saturdays by 1964, the station
ing served by four other trains daily in
ch direction. After lying empty the
ilding has now been converted into a
use and the space between the
atforms converted to a garden.

North Cornwall Line - OTTERHAM

The bleak and windswept location of Otterham was near the line's summit of 8((feet above sea level and was some two miles from the village of the same name b did serve the small seaside resort of Crackington Haven. Pine trees seen on th left were planted to afford the station site some protection from the fury of Atlantic gales. The former overbridge carrying the main A39 road has already been demolished in this view with the road running directly across the former trackbe The local hamlet still goes by the name of Otterham Station forty years on.

North Cornwall Line - DELABOLE

Delabole, with its massive slate quarry, wa an important source of freight revenue for the line and it is fitting that the main buildir was clad with the local product. The statio seen here in boarded up condition has definitely seen better days though it still retains its typical Southern concrete fencing, product of the Exmouth Junction Works. On my last visit to the site in the m 1990s it was occupied but was being engulfed by a new housing estate called "The Sidings".

...ne of the stations on this line that was rather optimistically named, being some four miles away down steep and narrow country ...nes from the village of its title. Used initially as offices for a nearby fertiliser store the building has been renovated and used as ...base for restoring Lotus cars.

1965	DMUs introduced to North Cornwall lines
10-1966	Closure of Okehampton – Bude / Wadebridge line

North Cornwall Line - **TRELILL TUNNEL**

The rarely photographed Trelill tunnel located between Port Isaac Road and St Kew Highway is seen in 1968. The southern portal shown here is plainer than the northern one which consists of a mixture of brick and stone. The tunnel was 330 yards long and surprisingly was one of the very few on the former SR lines west of Exeter given the nature of much of the terrain through which they ran.

The Royal Cornwall Show found a permanent site in Wadebridge in 1960 and invariably farm implements and exhibitors' wares came in by train. When the Household Cavalry took part in the 1960s whole trains of BR horseboxes transported their mounts from Knightsbridge via Kensington Olympia to North Cornwall. Here we see such a train waiting at Wadebridge in 1969.

WADEBRIDGE

Molesworth Street level crossing at Wadebridge on the Padstow extension was the scene of major traffic jams in former days. But all was quiet following cessation of passenger services to Bodmin Road in January 1967, road traffic being little inconvenienced by the occasional passage of freight wagons from Wadebridge Quay until April 1973. Wadebridge retained full load freight facilities until 4 September 1978, served by a daily train from St Blazey which also handled the onward carriage of china clay traffic brought down from Wenford Bridge by a Class 08 shunter.

Recovery of redundant track materials at Wadebridge is in evidence here with a rail mounted crane being located on the former down mainline and a bolster wagon and van on the up line. The island platform buildings have already been demolished though the main station building and canopy would survive to the present day housing the John Betjeman centre. The poet would arrive at this station from Waterloo to commence the final stage of his journey to his holiday home at Trebetherick by road. In his verse autobiography "Summoned By Bells" he describes his arrival thus –

> "…………………….Can it really be
> That this same carriage came from Waterloo ?
> On Wadebridge station where a breath of sea
> Scented the Camel valley ! Cornish air
> After Cornish rain, and silence after steam".

Well there is certainly silence now and has been for nearly 30 years since the final special train, arranged by the Bodmin Lions Club and consisting of DMUs B803 and B804, left to the accompaniment of the town band and exploding detonators on the afternoon of 17th December 1978.

st as a view of Meldon Viaduct is "de-
eur" for a book on SR lines in the
st Country, so no book on the
hered Arm would be complete
hout a shot of Little Petherick Creek
dge seen in the upper view. Following
ensive renovation in 2000/1, which
luded the provision of a concrete
ck, this structure was re-opened in
ne 2001 and now does duty on the
mel Trail cyclepath connecting
dstow and Bodmin. The lower view
ows the gorse covered rock cutting
the approach to Padstow station
ortly after the track was removed.

Tony Woodforth collection

Against a background of the beautiful Camel estuary, the extensive fish shed the majority of which have now been demolished, are evident in this view of Padstow taken after closure. Unfortunately most perishable goods traffic was lost for good after the damaging 1955 enginemen's strike. Although the track adjacent to the platform has been removed, rails, forming a couple of sidings, remain embedded in the concrete hardstandin
Tony Woodforth collect

Following closure of the North Cornwal line in October 1966, Padstow continue to see trains for a further three months until the Bodmin Road service also succumbed. The final timetable provide four through services to Bodmin Road, five on Saturdays, with one departure f Bodmin General, and two short working to Wadebridge, one of which was Saturdays only. Padstow, the end of th "Withered Arm" at 259 miles and 23 chains from Waterloo is seen in 1968 with a venerable single decker bus parked at the side of the building. The Metropole Hotel, destination of many former rail travellers, continues to brood over the site today which is largely give over to car parking, the station building housing local authority offices and toile

NBL Type 2 growls past Grogley Halt with a goods service from Wadebridge. A variety of inward traffic was handled including tiliser, basic slag and seed potatoes. The only outward traffic was slate dust from nearby Delabole Quarry which was carried in mer salt Presflo wagons a couple of which can be seen immediately behind the locomotive, the majority of these wagons ng destined for Tonbridge in Kent. This view is taken from the trackbed of the former Ruthern Bridge mineral line which closed December 1933. Freight services between Wadebridge and Boscarne Junction were withdrawn in September 1978.

-1-1967	Closure of Wadebridge – Padstow line
-1973	Quay sidings at Wadebridge closed
-12-1983	Launceston Steam Railway opened on part of old North Cornwall trackbed

Although only formed of standard SR concrete components, Nanstallon Halt presents an attractive picture in its rhododendron clad setting enhanced by the diminutive pair of level crossing gates and crossing keeper's house. Today, as with the remainder of the line, a cycle track runs where trains once did.

2-9-1978	Freight from Wadebridge via Bodmin Road ceased
3-10-1983	Wenford Bridge – Boscarne Junction closed for freight.

e short lived Boscarne Exchange platform built at a cost of £2,000 following revision of the timetable which saw the withdrawal
he long established steam services in May 1964. The replacement service consisted of an AC Cars 4 wheel railbus which
erated a shuttle from Bodmin North to Boscarne Exchange connecting with the DMU, or occasional Type 2 diesel locomotive
led, service from Bodmin Road to Wadebridge and Padstow. It would appear from this 1969 view that a second hand
neboard had been reused from Bodmin Road presumably to save money ! This had been covered with new signage reading
oscarne Junction change for Dunmere and Bodmin North". Although labelled Boscarne Junction it always appeared in the
etables as Boscarne Exchange platform. On 18 April 1966 the railbus shuttle was temporarily withdrawn, the ex SR station in
dmin being served by just two trains daily through the expedient of diverting the down Bodmin Road – Padstow services to run
Boscarne Junction where they had to reverse to Bodmin North where again they had to reverse to regain Boscarne Junction
d proceed to Padstow. This tedious process lasted less than 3 weeks when the MOT ordered BR to revert to the previous
angements. After a life of less than 3 years this platform closed with the closure of the line on 30 January 1967. In 1996 the
al Bodmin & Wenford Railway preservation society again reached this point and a new Boscarne Junction was born.

Bodmin General is seen in 1969 during its freight only existence under BR but during the time that the Great Western Society were allowed access to the site, permitted to keep their locomotive No 1363, a Churchward 0-6-0ST dock shunter of the 1361 class in the shed, to paint the signalbox and maintain some of the fabric of the buildings. The GWS subsequently moved out an before the present preservation society took over the signalbox and goods shed depicted here, together with the engine shed, were unfortunately demolished. Bodmin General was the site of a little known accident which occurred on 7th December 1961 when a train running in from Wadebridge, hauled by 4694, an 5700 Class Pannier Tank, collided with a diesel hauled empty stock working resulting in the unfortunate death of the steam locomotive driver.

...finish as we began at Salisbury, with a view of a Warship diesel this time at Bodmin Road. The brown and cream signboard ...ntinues to proclaim the junction status of Bodmin Road station although the date is 1969. Two years previously one could still ...ange trains here for Bodmin, Wadebridge and Padstow. With the North Cornwall line having closed in October 1966 this was ... sole rail connection to the former LSWR outpost but only lasted for some three months. A maroon liveried Warship is seen ...gaged in some desultory shunting with a solitary van in the up platform. China clay from Wenford Bridge was routed via ...dmin Road until complete closure of the line on 3rd October 1983. Today of course one can again change at Bodmin Parkway, ...it has been called since November 1983, for a rail journey to Bodmin General and Boscarne Junction and who knows one day ...haps Wadebridge or even Padstow may again be reached by rail. Until this comes to pass an hourly bus connection suffices ...m the station approach which still serves the furthest outpost of The Withered Arm.

RENAISSANCE

The story of the Southern Region's lines west of Salisbury over the past 45 years has not presented a totally negative picture. There have been some encouraging signs of development, some of which have been realised whilst some remain at varying stages from serious proposition to pipedream.

ACHIEVEMENTS

3-5-1971	Reopening of Sidmouth Junction station as Feniton
18-5-1983	Reopening of Pinhoe station
3-10-1983	Templecombe station re-opened
24-3-1986	Opening of Tisbury loop at cost of £435k
12-6-1993	New DMU depot opened at Salisbury, introduction of Class 159 units
1997	Okehampton station refurbished and Okehampton – Exeter reopened for special summer Sunday train
2-4-2000	Services operated from Okehampton – Meldon Viaduct (Dartmoor Railway)
5-2004	Sampford Courtenay station reopened

Today one would be hard pressed to locate the site of the station at Lydford Junction covered as it is in reed gorse and bushes. This 1970 view, taken shortly after track removal on the former SR mainline, shows the platforms used by the WR service from Plymouth to Launceston in the foreground. Although this line closed to passengers in 1962, freight traffic from Launceston and Lifton's Ambrosia creamery was brought out via the connection at Lydford Junction until February 1966. One of the more challenging schemes for the future is the reinstatement of the link southwards from Okehampton towards Plymouth so short-sightedly closed in 1968. Not only would this reunite local communities in North and South Devon but more importantly would provide a useful diversionary route when the coastal route at Dawlish is blocked.

FUTURE ASPIRATIONS

Reinstatement of Barnstaple – Instow – Bideford line (Bideford & Instow Railway Group).

Okehampton – Exeter plans for new interchange at Yeoford Junction to link with Tarka line and possible Park & Ride facility at Okehampton and resumption of commuter services.

Reopening of Bere Alston – Tavistock line with new Parkway station south of Tavistock. Possible long term reopening to Okehampton providing a useful diversionary route when sea wall route at Dawlish closed.

Reopening of Boscarne Junction – Wadebridge – possibly Padstow in the longer term. (Bodmin & Wenford Railway).

Possible reopening of Wenfordbridge – Boscarne Junction for freight traffic.

Launceston Steam Railway – current limit of operations from Launceston is 2.5 miles towards Egloskerry 2ft gauge. (Possible future extension).

Seaton Tramway – Colyton (current limit) possible extension to Seaton Junction and connection to mainline.

Redoubling of Salisbury – Exeter line.

Sidmouth – Feniton re-opening.

Lyme Regis – Axminster re-opening (Failed Minirail scheme) New scheme.